Big Machines

Ride Rails!

Catherine Veitch

Raintree is an imprint of Capstone Global Library Limited, a company incorporated in England and Wales having its registered office at 7 Pilgrim Street, London, EC4V 6LB – Registered company number: 6695582

www.raintreepublishers.co.uk
myorders@raintreepublishers.co.uk

Text © Capstone Global Library Limited 2015
The moral rights of the proprietor have been asserted.

Edited by Helen Cox Cannons and Kathryn Clay
Designed by Tim Bond and Peggie Carley
Picture research by Mica Brancic and Tracy Cummins
Production by Helen McCreath
Originated by Capstone Global Library Ltd
Printed and bound in China by Leo Paper Group

ISBN 978 1 406 28459 1
18 17 16 15 14
10 9 8 7 6 5 4 3 2 1

British Library Cataloguing in Publication Data
A full catalogue record for this book is available from the British Library.

Acknowledgements
We would like to thank the following for permission to reproduce photographs:

Alamy: © Matthias Scholz, 8, 9,© Peter Titmuss, 14, 15; Getty Images: NY Daily News Archive/Debbie Egan-Chin, 18, 19, Stone/Robin Smith, front cover; Newscom: AFP PHOTO/Stan HONDA, 21, STAN HONDA/AFP/Getty Images, 18; Rex Features: City AM/Micha Theiner, 12, 13; Shutterstock: jiawangkun, 4, 5, 22c, back cover, Tatiana Makotra, 16, 17, 22a, back cover, Wayne0216, 6, 7, 22d; Six Flags Great America: 20; SuperStock: age fotostock, 10, 11, 22b.

Every effort has been made to contact copyright holders of material reproduced in this book. Any omissions will be rectified in subsequent printings if notice is given to the publisher.

All the Internet addresses (URLs) given in this book were valid at the time of going to press. However, due to the dynamic nature of the Internet, some addresses may have changed, or sites may have changed or ceased to exist since publication. While the author and publisher regret any inconvenience this may cause readers, no responsibility for any such changes can be accepted by either the author or the publisher.

Contents

Some words are shown in bold, **like this.** You can find out
what they mean by looking in the glossary.

Big Boy locomotive

Big Boy was a huge train, or **locomotive**. It could pull up to 120 **freight cars** at once.

Big Boy 4012 is now on display at a railway museum.

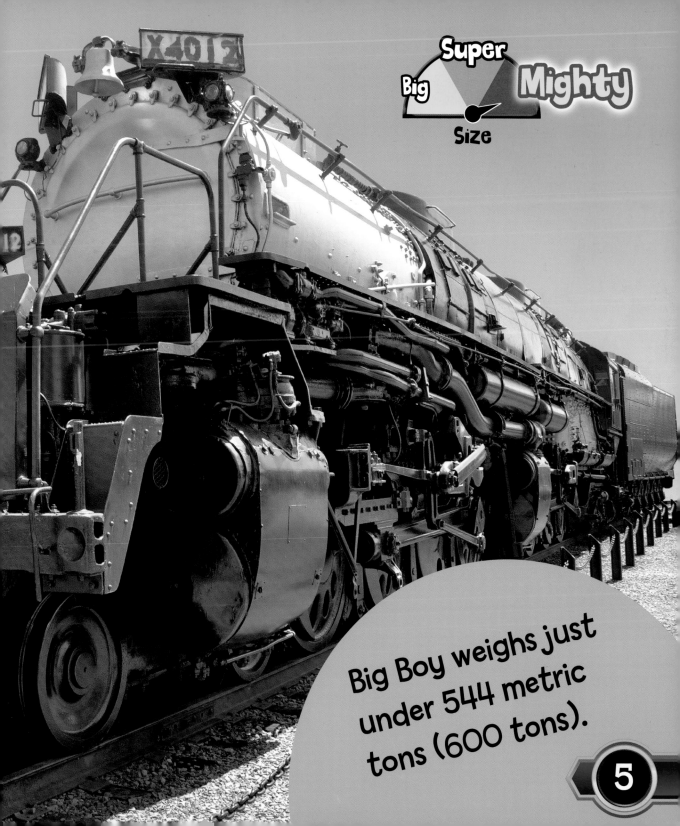

Big Boy weighs just under 544 metric tons (600 tons).

Bullet train

Bullet trains are fast **passenger** trains. Their **streamlined** shape helps them travel quickly.

Tunnels have been built for trains to travel straight through mountains!

Big **Super** **Mighty**

Size

The Taiwan High Speed Rail reaches speeds of 300 kilometres (186 miles) per hour.

Railway snowplough

Railway snowploughs can be as tall as houses. The driver climbs a ladder attached to the side of the machine to get in.

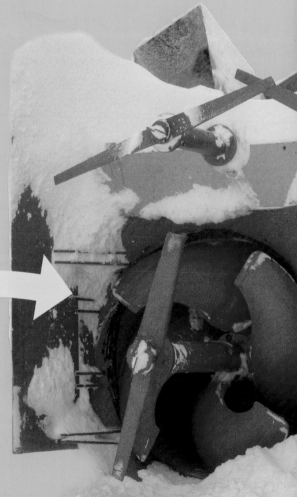

Huge metal blades push snow off the tracks.

Hanging train

This train is not upside down. It's hanging from a track!

Hanging trains were first built in Germany more than 100 years ago. There was no room for a railway track on the ground.

Eurostar

Eurostars travel under the sea
between England and France.
Builders started
building the
tunnel from
each end.
Amazingly,
they met
in the middle!

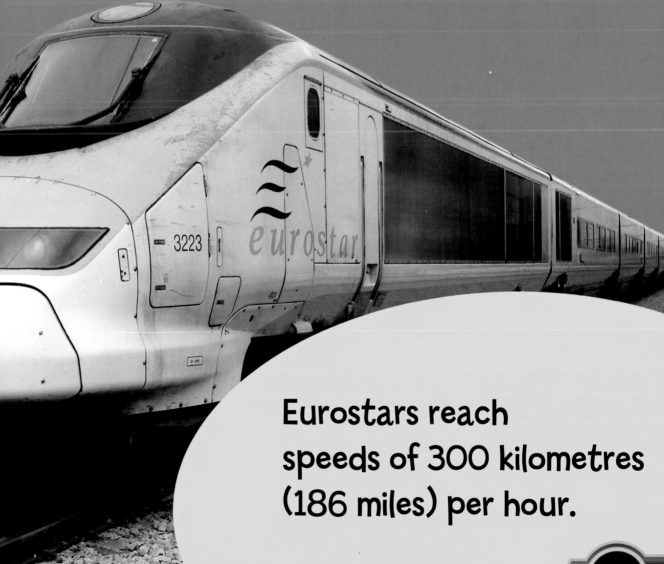

Eurostars reach
speeds of 300 kilometres
(186 miles) per hour.

Bilevel rail car

Bilevel rail cars are trains that have two levels. Passengers can eat, sleep and shower on these trains.

Size

Bilevel rail cars are also called double-decker coaches.

Monorail

A train that has one track is called a **monorail**. Many big cities have monorails above the ground.

02

China has the longest monorail track in the world. It is 167 kilometres (104 miles) long.

Roller Ride

Kingda Ka in New Jersey is the tallest roller coaster in the world.

Big Super Mighty

Size

Kingda Ka zooms around a track at speeds up to 128 miles (206 kilometers) per hour.

19

Largest Wooden Roller Coaster

Goliath at Six Flags Great America • Built in 2014

Tallest drop...... 55 metres (180 feet)

Steepest drop ... 85 degrees

Speed........... up to 116 kilometres (72 miles) per hour

Largest Steel Roller Coaster

Kingda Ka at Six Flags Great Adventure • Built in 2005
Tallest drop...... 127 metres (418 feet)
Steepest drop ... 90 degrees
Speed.......... up to 206 kilometres (128 miles) per hour

Quiz

How much of a Machine Mega-Brain are you?
Can you match each machine name to its correct photo?

**Big Boy • hanging train
bullet train • monorail**

1

2

3

4

Check the answers on the opposite page
to see if you got all four correct.

Glossary

freight car the part of a train that carries goods or cargo

locomotive the railway car that holds the engine to pull the train

monorail a railway that runs on one rail, usually high above the ground

passenger a person who rides on an aeroplane, train or other vehicle

streamlined designed to move easily and quickly through air or water

Find out more

Books

The Usborne Big Book of Trains, Megan Cullis (Usborne Publishing Ltd, 2013)

Train (DK Eyewitness Books), John Coiley (DK Publishing, 2009)

Websites

www.bbc.co.uk/learningzone/clips/trains-are-fantastic/11185.html
www.nrm.org.uk

Index